Joseph A. Dandurand

Hear and Foretell

BookLand
press

Published by BookLand Press
15 Allstate Parkway, Suite 600
Markham, Ontario L3R 5B4
www.booklandpress.com

Printed and bound in Canada

Front cover image © Bowie15

Library and Archives Canada Cataloguing in Publication

Dandurand, Joseph A., author
    Hear and foretell / Joseph A. Dandurand.

(Canadian Aboriginal voices)
Poems.
Issued in print and electronic formats.
ISBN 978-1-926956-96-1 (pbk.).--ISBN 978-1-926956-98-5 (pdf).--
ISBN 978-1-926956-97-8 (epub)

    I. Title. II. Series: Canadian Aboriginal voices

PS8557.A523H43 2015   C811'.54   C2015-900316-4
                                        C2015-900317-2

ONTARIO ARTS COUNCIL
CONSEIL DES ARTS DE L'ONTARIO
an Ontario government agency
un organisme du gouvernement de l'Ontario

Canada Council Conseil des arts
for the Arts du Canada

We acknowledge the support of the Canada Council for the Arts, which last year invested $157 million to bring the arts to Canadians throughout the country. We acknowledge the support of the Ontario Arts Council (OAC), an agency of the Government of Ontario. We acknowledge the financial support of the Ontario Media Development Corporation for our publishing activities.

Table of Contents

I Belong

I am no one
an afterthought
I am forgotten
to those who used
all of me.

I am the pathetic poet
who burns
but never ends.

it is the words
that appear before you
here in this flow
of tears.

this is who I am not
I am not breathing
the free air given to us
I am not
the lover I used to be.

the only thing
I know is
that the poet
is long gone
in a book like this one
turn the page
and
believe me.

The Kwantlens

I had to open a building
this morning for a crew
they were going north
into our territories
up in a place called
Stave Lake.

they will be digging for
stone tools
pieces of our
lost
puzzle.

who are we?

the Kwantlens.

a pitiful number of 90
that once numbered
in the thousands.

smallpox epidemic
wiped us out
80% of us sick
died
tortured
by illness
one sneeze
and it was over.

here now we dig
for our stones
ancient signs
that we once
lived further north
than this island.

here we are centuries
of pieces
of torn up
families.

quietly my son
goes to the water
and skips a stone
that will be found
a thousand years
from now
in a land
not
forgotten.

A Place Called Kwantlen

It's 7 am
throw net out
easy right?

wait
wait
watch
watch
August 4th
no sockeyes
no fish
where are they?

this is 10 thousand years later
and I am
as we all are
a part
of the people
the Kwantlen
most of us
like other river tribes
are rag tag people
of an ancient tribe
language is gone
land is gone
fish are gone
empty abused mind
of mine
gone.

but this is paradise
on this earth
at this time
for me
because
I have the dream of fish
and it is enough
to make me real
in this imaginary
place
called Kwantlen.

Simple Words

we raise our hands up to those
who walk the walk
talk the talk
they are so great
in how they come into a room
and save us with their words.

old ones are the best
they've seen it all
80 years some of them
they sit in the front
so close to the earth.

that's where we belong
in the earth and not above it
as we destroy it with our
need to eat
devour the earth
devour the gifts.

these gifts adorn our walls
images of the past
old time
old ones sitting
so close to the earth.

we buried another elder
and the sunshine
made our tears
warm.

the old ones
we raise our hands in the air
thank you
for
such
simple
words.

Friends Last Never

46 years I've been here
October 31, 1964 out east I arrived
in the Bethlehem of a cold nation.

the old man an air force man
smoked his cool menthol outside
as my mother screamed in agony
of my birth.

I watched all three of my kids
come out and cry for me to cradle
them.

I am and will always care for my kids
it's a chore but I drink it up.

no friends call or offer help
you get that if you are
a reclusive-troubled-manic-depressive.

I spend most days
waiting to hear a door opening
and the angel you threw out
into the streets
to return.

she never will
you are destined to die
quietly as you fold laundry
make lunches
walk to school
kiss them goodbye.

this is the dramatic scene
of a friendless
half
good
poet.

Murderous Fear

I've been hiding for about a week
as there was a murder on this little rez
I am afraid of simple life
now I am afraid to go out
afraid to leave my kids.

fear real fear
murderous fear
grips me.

me: broken old poet.

cold feet
put a hat on
feel better
feel safe.

I can smell the spirits
in the air
and I know the fish are coming
because you can smell them too.

song birds with new voices
sing outside
where I hide the fact
that I smoke like a dying
man's last wish.

the fear yes the fear of death
keeps me inside and I am
perfectly at home
in my home.

a sick child keeps me at home and
that's a good excuse.

so far we've done chicken pox
and pink eye and colds and the flu
and all of it keeps me inside
making chicken noodle soup
and reaching out
to anyone who can
understand me.

me: sore hand from
hacking out this poem
about fear and a sore throat
from way too many smokes.

I take my hat off and listen
to some music: AC/DC and their
good guitar.

as the day ends I hear the sweet
songs of song birds and I
listen to the fear in their voices.

the fear
the murderous fear
keeps us all
inside where it is safe.

me: finished and cold
so I put on a hat to hide myself
yes myself
the greatest fear of it all.

Afterthought Memories

where is the war?
where do priests go when they touch
little boys?

where are the nuns who
beat me and stepped on me
and controlled me?

this is not a poem for
carnivals and happy places
nor is this the perfect life
filled with pictures
of happier times.

people keep asking me for pictures
but I do not like being in a picture
and there is nothing mysterious
or sacred
as to why.

I am a picture.

this etched face
this empty heart
this portrait of a hack writer.

the fridge makes a noise
the uncaring listen into my home
wondering who I am.

don't ask
and no pictures please
leave me alone
to write pictures
like this one.

a landslide
of afterthought
memories
taken
and
tossed.

Spring Laughing

I wish I was in love again
good love
playful love
but I know the end
like the end
I just
went through.

what is love?

such a word
such a kick in
the ass.

I would welcome her
into my bed
and we both would be shy
unknowing
complicated.

we would devour each other
under sheets
ashamed of our own bodies
as they touch
and torture.

outside the frogs sing
at night down at the river
as an owl passes by
hunting.

the almost full moon
turns colours as
black and blue clouds
shade it.

the frogs sing because winter
is over and the fires that burned
up and down the river
no longer burn
as the smoke rises into
a cool mad night
and then we know
that spring is here.

love and pain
the frog and the owl
a lost voice
cowers beneath
the blankets
ashamed
yes
ashamed
of
touches.

I Love Books

I got one in the mail
an anthology
with one of my plays
plus a cheque for a
hundred bucks.

spent it on food and smokes
and gas for the car.

good to be in books
you get your name printed
and the day you were born
and soon to be the
day you died.

I love books because
they make a good place
to put my cup of coffee.

I am working on a new book
and it is a rough start
like all my books
and I am glad when
they are complete
then I rest
and hide some more
and I die some more.

a kitten sleeps on my
writing chair and she will
not let me sit down.

outside it is too noisy
inside my head it is too noisy
and the kids are bouncing
off the walls.

I need to sit
but the kitten
says no
and the poems are gone
gone until I can sit
and remember
until I can let go
until I can
allow it.

My Chest Hurts

this is another day
and we are so lucky.

I read Bukowski
and understood that he had cats
and I have cats.

Mr. Tess a 12 year old
slayer of river rats
inbred rabbits
every type of bird
snakes
squirrels
and he is so cute.

Miss Pearl our kitten
little miss mischief
she has learned to jump
on the kitchen counter
and she feeds on
last night's fish
spaghetti
lean steak
prawns
and she is so cute.

this is a day
when my chest hurts
because of too many smokes
that I throw away
outside and litter the earth
but I will rake them up
in the months to come.

this is a day
when nothing
that was supposed to happen
happened.

days go to nights
and even though
I do not drink
but I wish for a cold glass
of beer.

I would sip
it slow
as the cats murder
and the cats clean
last night's plate.

yes this is a day
and a night
to remember
as my chest hurts
and cats meow
their cuteness.

Slamming Poems to Paper

what's wrong with me?
does anyone know?
care?

if you know
could you call me late at night
when I am up slamming
poems to paper?

this pen feels so good
in my hand
and I have an empire
full of poems
and a play inside of my head
and I have the opening scene
and I have a story.

I want my arms tattooed
I love the pain
and my psychiatrist laughed at me
and told me
I was crazy.

so do not call me and tell
me I am insane
because aren't
we all?

I love and I love
and still I sit here
with this awesome pen
and I shred ink into images
and my hand cramps
as I get it all down.

I know now
yes I do
I remember when I was
a small boy
I fell on my head
and entered the world
unprotected and all
the monsters
found me
touched me
beat me down to where
I am.

I am
ugly
alone
mean
crazy
bored
unfulfilled
as the moon
changes
and becomes
another monster
and I hide
yes I do
hiding my life
in a house
on an island
too far
from love
and serenity.

Knocking

I read some good poems
about nothing at all.

they were better than mine.

song changes
the guitar rips
into the first day of spring.

I celebrate alone
like the dead poet forgotten but
still able to crank words
to page.

out in the yard
skittish birds
dance the dance.

I look beyond all of this
burn a cigarette
the smoke guides the guitar
as the song changes again.

in my empty house
you can imagine
all the ghosts
as they dance the dance.

the guitar stops
and then there's a knock
at my door.

no one is there
as this poem
becomes
all
too
familiar.

I Stare at Myself

I wish I had a new love
she would call
I would listen to her torment.

how do they find me?

I am free
kids are at their mom's
finally a break
I stare at myself
I stare at the pile of dishes
the laundry
the dust
yeah the dust.

I dream of a new love
and I dust myself off.

I hope she is cute
but I know
I will see the decades
of failure.

we would promise
to have a baby.

perhaps a new life
will blow the dust
that covers a broken heart.

here I sit
as a love dog
a dog man dog
who barked at too many
times of tragedy
and now the growl
of this time in my life
is much too soft
to scare them
away.

Burning Emptiness

I burn another smoke
I don't even like them anymore
I am going to quit
I started last August when
I caught all that fish.

it was hot and it was
burning my skin
and all I wanted
was a cigarette
something to calm me down
now they make me sick
to my stomach.

I hate them
they hate me
they control me
I hate them
they hate me
over and over I burn another
not even sure why
they taste best with a cup of coffee
any other time they just
burn into emptiness.

I could sip a glass of Jack Daniels
but we all know how that ends
it ends in a bad poem
about jail and violence
so light up
brothers and sisters
and think of me
as another
and another
flame of burning emptiness.

Tormented Souls

we laugh beyond laughter
two tormented souls
though not Christians
we believe this life
to be filled with memories
of a past abuse
both of us silly
standing there laughing
at nothing funny
to anyone else
on this corner
bank of a river
we stand
holding each other
breathing in the warmth
of this life that we have
been given
but by who
our parents?
it is when we question
ourselves
and our blame
of the other
that becomes unfunny
for me and I realize
that I am
the deathless poet
and death
is only
two poems
away.

At the River

the edges of the river fall
like the golden wings of a man
too close to the sun.

an eagle whistles at me
at my madness
this lucky predator
on a branch too high
for me to climb.

the cotton trees soak up
the March rains
as the west coast is
safely covered and protected
from disaster and war.

the river backs up
it looks so ugly when it slows
as the black birds
chase the eagle
trying to poop
on him and his wondrous wings.

the fire out back is gone
the wind is gone
the rain is gone
the eagle disappears
and the river moves forward now
back to the ocean
and the river is beautiful again.

the end is near
the pretty end
the last breath of life
as
the edges
of the river
fall.

Uprising

I hate the city
it lingers
it keeps you
escape to the ocean
fall to the bottom
let the sturgeon
dine upon me
I hate war
seen them all
world war two
parents took me to Dachau
when I was nine
the taste of death
still in my mouth
Vietnam
the bombs
drip the hell
the rice burns
I love rice
all the other wars
bomb
hate
love
it kills me
slower
than
any war could
I hate the smell of death
I hate the things that
stick to the back of your throat
rotten fish
death
war
cities

I hate the fact
that
I know
how
to
spell
hate.

Blue and Black Skies

today the sky
went blue to black
then back to blue.

a train whistled by
going east carrying
empty coal cars.

I cried
like every day
the tears fell when
a good tune came
on my car radio.

I passed the masses
all of us squinting
into the blue hot sky
as the sun got
in a nuclear way.

there is disaster
and happiness around me
there is pain
and there is lust.

the cat cries
his cry as I sip
a hot cup of Tims.

the sky darkens
and the night falls
and I cried
yes
this hardened
loser
cried
as skies
black and blue
slept.

Condemned Phone

my phone rings
I do not answer it
you are no good
you are a liar
you are a cheat
listen to me and my worries
listen to what I have.

I tell her to call him
and not me and I hang up
she calls back
and condemns me.

oh lord
what have I done to deserve this?

I guess I said
I love you.

those words place me upon a hill
facing the snow-capped mountains
that are shaped like ears.

I scream and the mountain ears hear me
and they do not answer me.

I do not answer the phone
when it rings the next time
it is the same time every day
and when I do answer
I roll down the hill
land on my feet
as the ringing
of the phone
is heard only
by the ears
of a faraway
mountain.

Pizza Box Pyramid

the kitten turns sideways
tail up coming at me
and then realizes I feed her.

food to bowl
tail down
crunching dry food
a cool sip of water
I feed the little thing.

in my garage
a pile of empty pizza boxes
stacked way too high to the heavens
teeters and one falls
and scares the kitten
who turns sideways
and stares at the empty box.

also in the garage
there are of course memories
of a love affair way too lost to fix
it becomes a pile here
and a pile there
as I take all the pictures of her
and put them in a corner
not as elaborate as the boxes
of empty
eaten
pizza.

I close the door
and the kitten meows
but I have turned sideways
tail up
defiant
to any
pile
of love
cold love
uneaten.

Rez Fairytale

an eagle sits on the highest branch
a seagull glides up river in
search for little fish
the sun hides
the wind hides
droplets of fine rain
shower the dried dirt road.

worms hide
crickets hide
an ugly looking rabbit
taunts its existence
as my 12 year old black and white
cat watches the rabbit from above.

this is a rez fairytale
and I am the little old man
scratching poems
as I remember my granny
who died decades ago
as her liver said
one more drink
is all you have left.

she had 17 kids
she became angry
wouldn't you?

the eagle is hiding
I look for a free feather
a sign that
I belong
in this story.

the sun hides
the earth hides
and the jam
on my buttered toast
glistens
in a morning
in a home
on a dried
dirt
road.

Start the Fire

rain falls (I live in BC)
always a bit of wind
so even if you duck away
the weather finds you.

my mom came over
with cat food
cookies
and a case of root beer
for the kids.

this is a good day
I feel alive
in an unlit fire
of life
and it's been this way
too long.

the dust on my mantle
is as thick as the dust
that covers me.

I am sitting here
waiting for a lovely woman
to wipe me clean.

I decide to light a fire
and the cracking wood
is the only sound in my
empty room of dust.

rain falls (you know why)
puddles
song birds
the world rotates
I stare into the fire
trying to see
the beauty
in who I am.

the smoke rises
and goes up into the sky
and I see myself laughing
and this memory
gives me
a moment to cherish
as the wood
that burns
perishes
not to dust
but
ashes
to ashes.

New Play

I am working on a new play
and I tell everyone that
as if it keeps me alive.

I write plays in my head first
and some come to me and I store
them and they are
the beginning
of the end.

this new play has three certain scenes
the opening
the middle
the end
yes
the end
came to me
and I will keep it
to myself
until I write it down.

this is how they come to me
as images
as stories
as gifts
and I store them
inside me until
I have no more room
and I sit down
and explode
and rip my mind
unto sheets
of bloody
paper.

poems come from
a place
a feeling
like this poem
stolen
from a pocket
in my mind
and I do not know
who or what
will fill that space
as you will have to wait for
the
final
curtain
to
fall.

Saturday Night

lonely
we all get that
kids bouncing off the walls
kept them in all day and night
driving me to be normal.

house is a mess
I clean a pile here
and a pile there.

music is on
Marilyn Manson
The Beautiful People.

I am in a rhythm now
the pen flows
my mind escapes
Saturday night
on an island
in a village
down the road
from madness.

the coyotes
bark at a passing train
the earth goes quiet
there for a moment.

I change the song
and the pen flows
until the coyotes
parade down to the river
and drink the eternal waters
not of madness
but
the cool
wet
of calmness.

Cold Hands of Abuse

battery dead
everyone wants a picture
of my ugly mug.

I do not even
like looking
at myself.

why would anyone else?

they just want to laugh
feel good that age has
destroyed my beauty.

I used to be cute
but with that came
the men who abused me.

bastards!

I fall into a hole
and they cannot find me
as I pull up my pants
and I am a
victorious animal to be reckoned with.

in that hole I am
good and warm
as the moon comes out
and the men
are all dead and gone.

stupid men
how did they know
that decades later
I would still feel
their touch and
their cold hands
of abuse
would appear on
every
picture
of my
ugly
mug.

Wet Cigarette

I've lived in a desert
I've lived on a glacier
I've lived in a cave
I've even lived on a boat.

not that
that means much.

the world is at war
and I have one smoke left but
the west coast rains have soaked
me to the skin.

I try and light it
but no good
as my last request
in a world at war
has been wasted.

the eagles sing
a good tune
as the devil dances
and the world destroys
itself again
and again.

I've died a thousand times
I've died in a cave
I've died on a mountain
I've even died in a pool
of sweat as my lighter
flares and I smoke
the good smoke.

farewell as the world
destroys itself
and the war machine
falls like
a wet smoke
in a wet cave
somewhere past
this last wish
of mine.

Lovers

there have been good ones
sad ones
crazy ones
and then I speak
and all of them run away.

wouldn't you?

am I so terrible?

I go in with passion
upon my lips
as I caress them
as I love them.

today I have no lovers
only memories of goodbyes
and I wonder who is loving
them all now.

I curl up on an empty bed
hugging myself
trying to feel a sensation that
is no longer there.

the window is closed
the blinds are down
the cats are sleeping
the room is empty
except for a frightened man
hiding his love
from lovers
who all walked away.

I open my mouth
to speak
to save myself
but the words
are all empty
yes
my
words
are
empty.

Like a Slug

a slug moves across my back porch
where I go every morning to hide
the shame of smoking again.

it takes its time sliding its way
across the cedar planks.

this is me I thought to myself
as I inhaled and felt the burn
in my throat.

this is me
the slowness
the calmness
like death
slow
unlike life
which is quick
quick
and over
yet we try and try
to bend it
yet we try
to break it.

a slug leaves a trail of slime
like memories of my life
as I light another smoke
and breathe
feel the burn
write a poem
watch the sky
another day gone by
this wonderful gift of life
this need to carry on
across cedar planks.

this is the man I am
taking it slow now
because I understand
I get it.

life is too short
take it slow
and pray
the birds
do not
eat
us.

Break the Silence

kids are at their mom's
the house is too quiet
I find myself making unneeded noises
clapping
applauding to an empty stage
whistling
"stop whistling"
my father told me
over and over again
"you can't whistle!"

the symphony in my head
was pure agony for the old man
who had just quit smoking
poor soul.

I work away at some new poems
as poetry is much quieter than
off-key whistles.

to me the words leave my lips
and hit the air and break
the silence.

I need the noise of the kids
even the noise on my worst days
and I love the teasing they throw at me
they even hide and creep up on
me knowing it will hit a nerve
eventually.

I turn off the lights
and try to fall asleep
only to awake to whistling
a bad tune
and I run to get a pen and paper
and write it down.

one two three
one two three
the words like angels
like children
pure and needed
as I remember they will
be home in two more days
and in two more days
the violins
will
scream.

Taken

I am taken
again
fell right into the same hole
that I knew was there
and like the lover-fool
I play so well
in this ugly affair
I climb out
and have a smoke
even though I quit
a week ago
and I take my meds
even though I stopped
two weeks ago
but I need to sleep
I need to remember
why I am here
and I need to not fester
as to why
I am not here.

I am taken
and the band plays on
and people run away
just as fast
as they came around
and I get a visit
from an old friend
and I know
he can see right through me.

as I am taken
I fall
into the same hole
but this time
I am unable
to climb out
and the hole
slowly closes
and
I
am
taken.

The Canyon Where...

cracks
in
the
road
birds
singing
screaming
an
old
forgotten
opera
amongst
themselves
echoes
of
distant
drums
treachery
and war
cries
out
to
this
place
called
Kwantlen
IR #6
on
the
river
towards
the
canyon

where
Gods
embrace
the
salmon
who
dance
the last dance
as
man
destroys
man
all
over
again.

Bone Necklace

given to me as a gift
as we remembered a good man
I do not wear it
but I touch it
and the magic comes
I can see things
that others would
not want to come inside
I allow the images
the dreams
thoughts
words
to come inside
you are welcome
here inside of me
the price you pay
is always painful
sometimes you
feel little
other times you
feel it all
and it takes away
a part of you
I do not wear
the gift
I allow it to come in
come on in
and sit with me brother
and have some tea
and cookies
you are welcome
I whisper to the dead
as they
cry

and
cry
not in sadness
no
the spirits
are celebrating
a simple gift
you are welcome
as I close the door
and another part of me
slips out
and goes to the other side
where they
cry
and
cry
and cry.

I Wish I Was

it is a simple sketch
of a God
to me it is perfect
to others it is
a poor scribble
red ink
on white paper
its hands held upward
and there are eyes
in its belly
its mouth is open
not in a scream
but in a song
it is the song
that we all have heard
so sweet
so genuine
it wears a hat
of wet red cedar
woven by
another God
the song
yes the song
it holds us
here on earth
we are connected
and if we let go
then we let go.

I let go
and I am falling
down into
emptiness
of who I am
and who I wish
I was
to be perfect
beautiful
loved by a God
or a woman
yes that is my song
and always has been
such a pretty song
as I fall into
a world where I
am perfect if only
for a moment
this moment
gives to me
hope
and when I land
I no longer hear the song
I walk back up
from this ugliness
and become
the angel
of
a
song.

Swollen Mind

to myself I tell people
that the inside of my
head feels like it is
swollen.

I could never say it
out loud because of fear that
they would look at
me funny as if
I was crazy.

it is true
the walls of my head
feel thick and bloated
not with nightmares
or wonderful dreams
but it feels like
there is no room there
for right or wrong.

it began when I was young
I remember my mind
being so swollen
that I could not
speak.

it is much easier now
because being alone
I have nothing
to say
to anyone
no words of
I love you
I hate you.

the swollenness
disappears
and I carry on.

today an eagle
flew so close over
my head that
it startled me
and I thanked the
eagle for reminding me
that even as I live alone
there is life
above me
that is so
wonderful.

I go inside of my home
and I thank the skies
and the eagles
for giving me
a life
though sometimes
swollen
a life with images
that
suffer
no
more.

I Stare

at old pictures
crumpled days
gone by
at lust
at pain
at vengeance
and none of it
makes any sense
at all.

I stare at my
eyes
they stare back
what they see
is a man of 47
a little boy
a suffering soul
a lost day
of searching for
that soft kiss.

I reach out
but there is no one there
I touch the moon
but it falls
behind blue-black clouds
I kiss the wind
but I taste the air
and it is warm
and it cleanses me.

I embrace this day
and I stare
at the mist of a wet
morning that fades
and I open my eyes
and I see that little boy
playing imaginary
games
all by himself
for hours
and then I close my eyes
and I see that old man
that lovely poet
as he
kisses the air
hugs a memory
and then the moon
climbs to the blue-black sky
and the night falls
and I stare into
the end of the day.

I stare until the moon
says no more
and I sleep and dream
of
a
kiss
soft
so soft
like the imagination
of a man
I am.

Washing Away

self-deception guides me
through the year
I walk to the water
strip naked
wade in
holler the coldness
count to ten
dunk myself
washing away my sins
there is someone or something
watching me
laughing at me
I get dressed
awoken by the
ice mountain waters
I drive back
into the present
a new man
I begin to see it more clearly
this is what I should do
this is what I am going to do
I breathe in a breath so fresh
it frightens me
it frightens that someone or something
will stop laughing
I enter a warm world
full of myself
the warmth of cold saves me
the ice of water tells me
I am divine
praise the lord
this sinner has become a saint
the laughter is an echo
the touch of a flame

barely teases me
the need to get out
drives me to want cold water
the cold water
calls to me
I go
again
up the mountain
past the laughter
of
someone
or something.

Good Luck Charm

a small frog
hugs the top part
of our front door
I tell the kids
it's good luck
they of course look
at me like I am
not sure what I am
talking about
this is a look
I get most of the times
when I open my mouth.

I want to tell them
that I know this
because I have
been here before
in a previous life
a life that was
so much easier
but I hold my tongue
and wait for the next
good luck charm
it comes in the form
of a death
of a friend
of my eldest daughter
she is truly hurt
and cries and I ask her
what happened
and she tells me her
young friend died
in a car crash
and I think hard and all

I can say to her
that this is life
and this is death
and to think of good things
of her friend
and of course
she looks at me
as if I know nothing.

later in the day
I sit here
like I sat here
in another life
that was easier
this time round
I have three children
looking at me
for the answers
and I tell them the best
that I can
this is life
this
is
life.

Suicidal Thought

no self-pity
suck it up
get on with it
you think you got it bad
these are words
to myself as I
dream of what it
would be like to
swing from the rope
in the back of my house
in my smokehouse
that should be hot
with smoke and the
smell of salted fish
it fades as do all suicidal thoughts
and the meds help but sometimes
all it takes is a sad song
a memory
the thought of blame
I blame you
and you
and you.

the house is silent
this pen is full of it
my dog sleeps
my cat devours a chipmunk
I pile my garbage out on the deck
another sad song
another reach for the rope.

I calm myself
the thought changes
to a dream
but what to dream of?
this is self-pity
I tell the world
can you not hear me?

I calm down
sip a coffee
smoke a cigarette
stare in the mirror
turn away from
these eyes of mine
what they have seen
what they will see
if only I could tell
the world
scream out loud for all
to hear
that I wish
to live one more day
even if I am
kissing
the
noose.

Hollow Ecstasy

buried a dream
cradled a sasquatch
briefly saw little people
as they ran away into a forest.

kissed an angel
touched the sun
pissed on fallen leaves
as they fell from the
heavens above.

loved a lover
tore my heart out
wore shoes with no socks
joined a circus
breathed fire while
horses danced.

paid my dues
forgot to buy milk
decided I am ok
lived once before
as a rattlesnake.

opened a book
tore out a page
broke a pencil
wrote a bad poem
about misery and laughter.

cut my hair
ate a whale
burned a nightmare
discovered that
no matter how hard
I try I still
have to talk
to someone.

barbecued fish
split wood
burned old news
about this
and that.

dove into the sea
kissed another lover
caressed the sins
of all those
bastards.

I went to the other side
talked to someone
tried to explain
that there wasn't much
left for me to do.

they kicked me out
I could smell cedar boughs
the wind blew cold in my face
which of course
I
had
changed.

Internal Graveyard

little brown birds peck at my house
they are winter chubby
they bounce around on my roof
eating bugs too cold to fly away.

there is a dark feeling outside
as winter comes into the doorway
and all the leaves are on the ground
and my lawn looks like a giant
unsolvable puzzle of lost dreams.

the white church on this island rez
sits empty as all the Indians
believe no more in a God that
punished them.

the stained glass windows are all boarded
up as our youngsters tossed stones through
the pretty pictures of all the saints
who died for our sins.

there is a glimmer of star-like skies
as rains create universe-like puddles
and the chubby brown birds
bathe in the waters of our lord.

they say we nailed him to a cross
but our little church has no cross
as our young people took it out
with one God killing stone.

the stone sits on the ground
surrounded by pretty flowers
that are no longer pretty
and they dry up and blow away
as all the sinners kneel
somewhere else.

somewhere past this internal graveyard
we hear a song to the God
who feeds too-cold bugs
to the angels
as they become chubby
and sleep the winter
of this island rez
two doors down
from the unsolvable puzzle
of ancient people
still here after centuries
of falling down
on our knees
we stand up
and pick up the pieces
of this
empty
unsolvable
dream.

We Are

the wind
the furnace
the phone
the empty
the dirty dishes
the coyote
the cat
the dog
the car
the truck
the boat
the filthy garage
the blowing rain
the broken fingertip
the new tattoos
the old tattoos
the straw
the cold drink
the owl
the slugs
the grass
the face
the eyes
the memories
the past
the lost
the poison
the meds
the liquor
the cigarettes
the pipe
the musty clothes
the chewed gum

the father
the son
the
holy
screams
of
we are
we are!

Stone Secrets

I knew a man who could turn me into a stone
I knew another man who could control the time
I met a girl who could make me cry
I met another girl who could make me laugh
I knew the far corners of this earth
and there once was a man who could
fly inside a room full of secrets.

I heard of this girl who could go
and come back as a quiet note
of forgiveness.

I've seen things that I cannot write about
I watched a grown man scream
and yell and throw stuff around a room
filled with secrets.

they say there are good things and bad things
they say this life is a good life but a hard life.

I've seen a woman heal a thousand faces
I've tasted a girl who wept while
I made love to her.

there once was a man who climbed
on top of his own life and came back down
and forgot who he was.

I saw a man and a woman live together
for 40 years and he died and she lived
and now he comes to her trying to climb
down and see if he can do it better
this time.

I know a girl who lives far away
on snow covered prairies
and she is for me
and this time
I will do it right
as I climb up the mountain
where the man made of stone
tells
me
a
secret.

Am I Allowed?

to miss my wife
walk alone
along a sidewalk
made of paper?

am I allowed
to brush off
everyone else's
problems
their petty
gripes eating
away each
other?

can I write poetry
can I practice my
solitude until there's
no more nights left
to be by myself
in this pity-filled
castle?

will I vanish
like a piece of
history already
forgotten?

am I to hold her
like in the old days
when we were afraid
of our own family?

will there be days
like this day
when the pen
changes white paper
to sentences of
what
where
when?

when will it end
this broken path
of paper-made
sidewalks?

I jump
up and down
trying to shake
her from my
mind
she has me
as pen and paper
create
another step
and I walk
and fall
and get up
and another step
to where?

only
the pity
knows.

Forward

to the back of the class
feeling good about
being abused
as handsome nuns
are slapping me
and I wonder
if they will also
go to hell
like the priest
who pulled
on
my
pee
pee.

My Smashed Head

thrown away
when I fell off some stairs
when I was four
smashed my head
was never the same
used goods
the first four years were ok
no complaints
the horror came later
the pain of the belt
a giddy priest
a hell-bent nun
older boys with guns
but it's all right
now I am here fuckers
missing my old lover
missing a dream
with this new life at 46
here I am
I keep all my pieces in the corner
inside the tossed piece of paper
is a new play about to be written
I will mail it
then I will be asked to accept the award
for the best writer in the world
with my smashed head
as I humbly thank no one
just me
and my four years
as golden
as yesterday.

Two Worlds

cold 10th day of a winter month
the ground is frosted
cloudless moment
tonight me and the kids
go up river to a gathering
this is who we are
living in two worlds
one world filled with candies and cake
another world filled with dreams and sadness
sorrow is a step to the other side
you can hear them crying
you can hear them crying to the sky
my little ones huddle on their blankets
they know the songs
they know the medicine
the other world is forgotten
as the candy and cake burn
it is time to travel
winter time
it is time to let it all go
holler to the spirits
that you have arrived
a man puts wood on the fire
as my little ones fall asleep
and dream of one world
a world and time
that tastes less and less
like candy and cake
a world that
hears the cries
of all our people
as the fire burns
and the night
listens.

Quiet Dinner Alone

I gave cats the leftovers
I eat alone
kids with their momma
anyone wants to come over
and breathe some of the air?

the silence gets me
the darkness gets me
the echo of laughter
well
it gets me the most.

the light comes through my skylight
I open my eyes and another day
begins
but what shall I do?

could go visit a friend
could stop at the bar
could listen to some music
could laugh out loud
could breathe all this extra air
could cry
could write a poem
if
only
I
could.

Hear and Foretell

her lips
her lips
I await our first kiss
as it has been so long since
I held a woman in my arms
that I believe I will be
awkward and might even
fall down.

her body
her body
I have always wanted her
and soon she will come
to see me
and I will devour her.

her whispers
her whispers
are like prophecies
of who I
will be.

her tears
her tears
will only fall
in happiness
as I caress her
and tell her
I love her.

the moment
the moment
we discover
a child inside
of her.

the birth
the birth
of our baby
and the cries
late at night
to be fed and clothed
and loved.

the dreams
the dreams
like this poem
come and go
as I fall and get
up in a
deep
deep
sorrow
as I realize
I am all alone
inside a mind
that teases me with
false hope.

the hope
the hope.

About the Author

Joseph A. Dandurand is a member of the Kwantlen First Nation located near the Fraser River, east of Vancouver. He works as the Heritage and Lands Officer for the Kwantlen territory and has been performing his duties for over 15 years. He studied theatre and direction at Algonquin College and at the University of Ottawa. He was a Playwright-in-Residence for the Museum of Civilization in Hull in 1995 and for Native Earth in Toronto in 1996. His previously published books include *Looking Into the Eyes of My Forgotten Dreams* and *Please Do Not Touch the Indians*. His poems have appeared in numerous journals and anthologies, including *An Anthology of Canadian Native Literature in English*. He has also authored a radio script which was produced by CBC Radio in 1999.